STARTING AMERICA

Thomas Jefferson and His Writings

BY PAT MᶜCARTHY

PEARSON
Scott
Foresman

Editorial Offices: Glenview, Illinois • Parsippany, New Jersey • New York, New York

Sales Offices: Needham, Massachusetts • Duluth, Georgia • Glenview, Illinois
Coppell, Texas • Ontario, California • Mesa, Arizona

Jefferson's Ideas

Thomas Jefferson was a man of many ideas. He was more modern in his thinking than many other people of his time. He believed in liberty for everyone. He was good at stating his ideas clearly in his writing. Much of our government is based on Jefferson's ideas. He wrote some of our country's most important documents.

Jefferson was born on April 13, 1743, at Shadwall, the family farm in Virginia. He had seven brothers and sisters.

When Jefferson was born, Virginia belonged to England. It was one of England's thirteen colonies in what is now the United States.

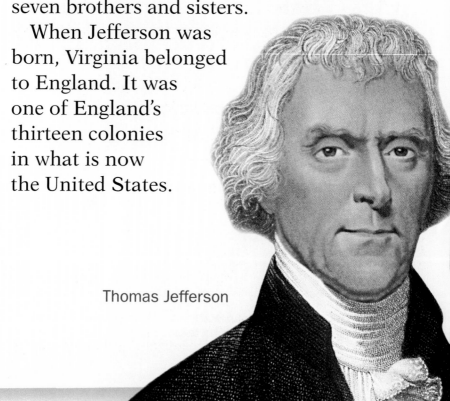

Thomas Jefferson

Jefferson's Education

When Jefferson was two years old, the family moved to a plantation. They were living there when Jefferson started school. There he learned to read, write, and do arithmetic. Jefferson's father later sent him to school to learn French, Greek, and Latin.

From his father, Jefferson learned to be independent. His father told him, "Never ask another to do for you what you can do for yourself."

When Jefferson was fourteen, his father died. Jefferson attended another school for two years. When he was sixteen, Jefferson went to the College of William and Mary. He made friends with a professor, Dr. William Small, who introduced him to people close to the governor.

William and Mary College

After two years Jefferson left college to study law with George Wythe, a well-known lawyer. The two men discussed important legal cases, and Jefferson read law books. He attended court to watch lawyers in action. Jefferson later wrote that Wythe was "my faithful and beloved mentor [teacher] in youth and my most affectionate friend through life."

Jefferson Enters Politics

Jefferson became a lawyer in 1767. Two years later he was elected to the House of Burgesses, Virginia's lawmaking body. Jefferson, like many other Virginians, was unhappy with British rule.

Jefferson studied law.

Jefferson Settles Down

In 1772 Jefferson married Martha Wayles Skelton. He built a house named Monticello on land he had inherited.

The colonists were becoming unhappy with British rule. They thought they should be free to make their own laws and be a **direct democracy**. They thought England had too much control.

In 1774 Jefferson wrote a booklet about the colonists' rights. In it he said that the English government did not have the right to make laws for the colonies since the colonists had no representatives. This booklet was called *A Summary View of the Rights of British America*.

Monticello

The Colonies Declare Independence

In 1774 a **council** called the First Continental Congress met in Philadelphia. Representatives from most colonies were there to discuss the problems with England.

The next year, the Second Continental Congress decided the colonies should declare their independence from England. A committee was chosen. They chose Jefferson to write the document.

Jefferson spent two weeks working on this document. He tried to express how most Americans were feeling. He explained his belief that when men tried to settle problems with those who ruled them and could not, they had the right to break ties with the ruling nation. He later said that the Declaration of Independence was meant to be "an expression of the American mind."

Preamble to the Declaration of Independence

Signing of the Declaration of Independence

The Congress passed the Declaration of Independence. It was signed on July 4 of 1776 and was read to the public on July 8.

The Colonies Fight for Independence

The colonies were now fighting the Revolutionary War to gain their freedom from England. The war would last eight years.

In 1777 Jefferson wrote another important document called the *Virginia Statute of Religious Freedom*. In this document Jefferson said that the government should not interfere with anyone's religious freedom. A person should have the freedom to believe and worship as he or she chose. Personal liberty was very important to Jefferson, and this can be seen in most of his writings.

In 1779 Jefferson was elected governor of Virginia. This was one of the worst times of Jefferson's life. It was his **responsibility** to keep the people of Virginia safe from the British attackers, but Virginia did not have enough money to buy the supplies or food that the colonial soldiers needed. The British attacked several places in Virginia and even controlled Monticello for a while. Many people blamed Jefferson for Virginia's problems.

Jefferson Returns to Monticello

Jefferson's time as governor ended before the war did. He went back to Monticello where he wrote a book about Virginia. It was published several years later.

Jefferson wrote a book about Virginia, along with many other documents.

The next year Jefferson's wife Martha died soon after the birth of their sixth child, Lucy. Jefferson was so sad that he would not come out of his room for three weeks. His daughter Martha was the only person he would allow into the room with him.

Jefferson Serves His Country

Jefferson, however, could not stay in his room forever. His country needed him, and Jefferson was willing to serve. He was elected to the new Congress in 1783 and wrote several important documents.

Soon Jefferson was asked to go to France to help John Adams and Benjamin Franklin make treaties with several of the nations of Europe, so the new United States could trade with them. Jefferson agreed to go.

Jefferson became good friends with John and Abigail Adams and their family. That friendship was a comfort to him when Jefferson received the sad news that his baby Lucy had died. Jefferson stayed in France for five years.

While Jefferson was in France, George Washington was elected as the first President of the United States. Washington asked Jefferson to be Secretary of State. Jefferson kept that job for three years, working to help the United States get along peacefully with other countries.

In 1796 Jefferson ran as a **candidate** for President but lost to his friend John Adams. That made Jefferson Vice President. He had a difficult time in this job because he and Adams did not agree on many things.

Jefferson as President

In 1800 Jefferson beat Adams in the presidential election. As President, Jefferson worked hard. He got up at five o'clock in the morning and spent several hours each day working at his desk. He held large dinners, and served his guests new foods, such as ice cream, peach flambé, and macaroni.

Thomas Jefferson

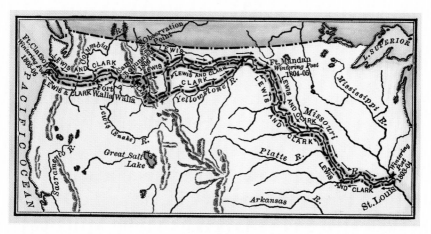

Lewis and Clark explored the new territory.

In 1803 Jefferson arranged for the United States to buy Louisiana from France. This huge territory stretched from the Rocky Mountains to the Mississippi River. The Louisiana Territory doubled the size of the United States.

Jefferson sent Meriwether Lewis and William Clark to explore the new territory and told them to take notes about the soil, plants, animals, and land. Lewis and Clark traveled eight thousand miles in a little over two years. They brought back many drawings, journals, and maps. People began moving west when they heard about the things Lewis and Clark had seen. This was the beginning of the westward movement in America.

Retirement from Politics

Jefferson decided not to run for President again. He was happy to return home to Monticello. He showed his feelings when he wrote to a friend, "Never did a prisoner released from his chains feel such relief."

Jefferson enjoyed spending time with his grandchildren and his many visitors, but sometimes he liked to spend time alone reading in his large library. He often said, "I cannot live without books."

The British burned the library in Washington, D.C. during the War of 1812. Jefferson offered his own library to replace it. This was the beginning of what is now the Library of Congress.

The Library of Congress, as it looks today.

This is the revolving bookstand that Jefferson invented. It let him read five books at a time!

In addition to being a reader and writer, Jefferson was an inventor. Most of his inventions were things that made everyday life simpler. He invented a revolving bookstand and a portable desk that he used to write the Declaration of Independence. He liked the macaroni he ate in France, so he invented a machine that would make macaroni. He also invented a new iron plow. Most plows were wooden, and it was difficult for them to cut through the hard clay soil. Jefferson's plow had an iron blade and made the work easier.

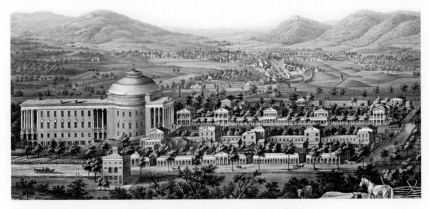
Jefferson founded the University of Virginia.

Jefferson's biggest project during his retirement was the founding of the University of Virginia. This was the first university that was not connected to any church. Jefferson believed education and religion should be separate, just as he believed religion and government should be separate. The university opened in March of 1835. Jefferson invited all the students to dinner at Monticello many times.

Jefferson's Death

Thomas Jefferson died at Monticello on July 4, 1826. The date was exactly fifty years after the signing of the Declaration of Independence. Jefferson was eighty-three years old. John Adams died that same day.

Thomas Jefferson was buried under a big oak tree on a hillside at Monticello. His wife Martha, his daughter Maria, and his sister Jane were buried nearby.

Of all his accomplishments, Jefferson was most proud of his writing. He designed his own tombstone and said he wanted these words and "not a word more" engraved on it. His tombstone reads:

HERE WAS BURIED

THOMAS JEFFERSON

AUTHOR OF THE

DECLARATION

OF

AMERICAN INDEPENDENCE

OF THE

STATUTE OF VIRGINIA

FOR

RELIGIOUS FREEDOM AND

FATHER OF THE UNIVERSITY

OF VIRGINIA

Glossary

candidate a person who runs for office

council a group of people who make laws and rules for a community

direct democracy government run by the people who live under it

governor a person elected as the head of a state in the United States

responsibility a duty; something that must be done